Romeo & Juliet

Retold by Anna Claybourne
Illustrated by Tom Morgan-Jones

WAYLAND
www.waylandbooks.co.uk

First published in 2015 by Wayland
Copyright © Wayland 2015

All rights reserved
Dewey number: 823.9'2-dc23

MIX
Paper from
responsible sources
FSC
www.fsc.org
FSC® C104740

10 9 8 7 6 5 4 3 2 1

ISBN: 978 0 7502 8114 0
eBook ISBN: 978 0 7502 8810 1
Library eBook ISBN: 978 0 7502 9360 0

Editor: Elizabeth Brent
Design: Amy McSimpson
Illustration: Tom Morgan-Jones

Wayland, an imprint of Hachette Children's Group
Part of Hodder & Stoughton
Carmelite House
50 Victoria Embankment
London EC4Y 0DZ

Printed in China

An Hachette UK company
www.hachette.co.uk
www.hachettechildrens.co.uk

CONTENTS

INTRODUCING
ROMEO AND JULIET

"Romeo, Romeo, wherefore* art thou Romeo!?" These famous words express Juliet's anguish that the boy she loves, Romeo, is from a family her parents hate. *Romeo and Juliet*, the ultimate story of doomed young love, is among Shakespeare's most popular plays, and one of the best-known stories of all time.

*In Shakespeare's language, "wherefore" means "why?"

Who was Shakespeare?

Today, we know William Shakespeare as one of the greatest writers ever. He lived around 400 years ago, working in London, England as an actor and playwright, and wrote nearly 40 plays. Although they may now sound old-fashioned, they are still read, performed and loved all over the world.

What's the story?

When Romeo Montague falls in love with Juliet Capulet, they know their parents will be furious. So they marry in secret, hoping to bring their feuding families together. But before long, it all goes horribly wrong, as Juliet's parents promise her hand in marriage to another man, and Romeo is drawn into a deadly street fight.

Read on to begin the fast and furious, touching and tearstained story of *Romeo and Juliet*...

Romeo and Juliet: Who's who?

At the start of every Shakespeare play is a list of characters, called the *dramatis personae*.

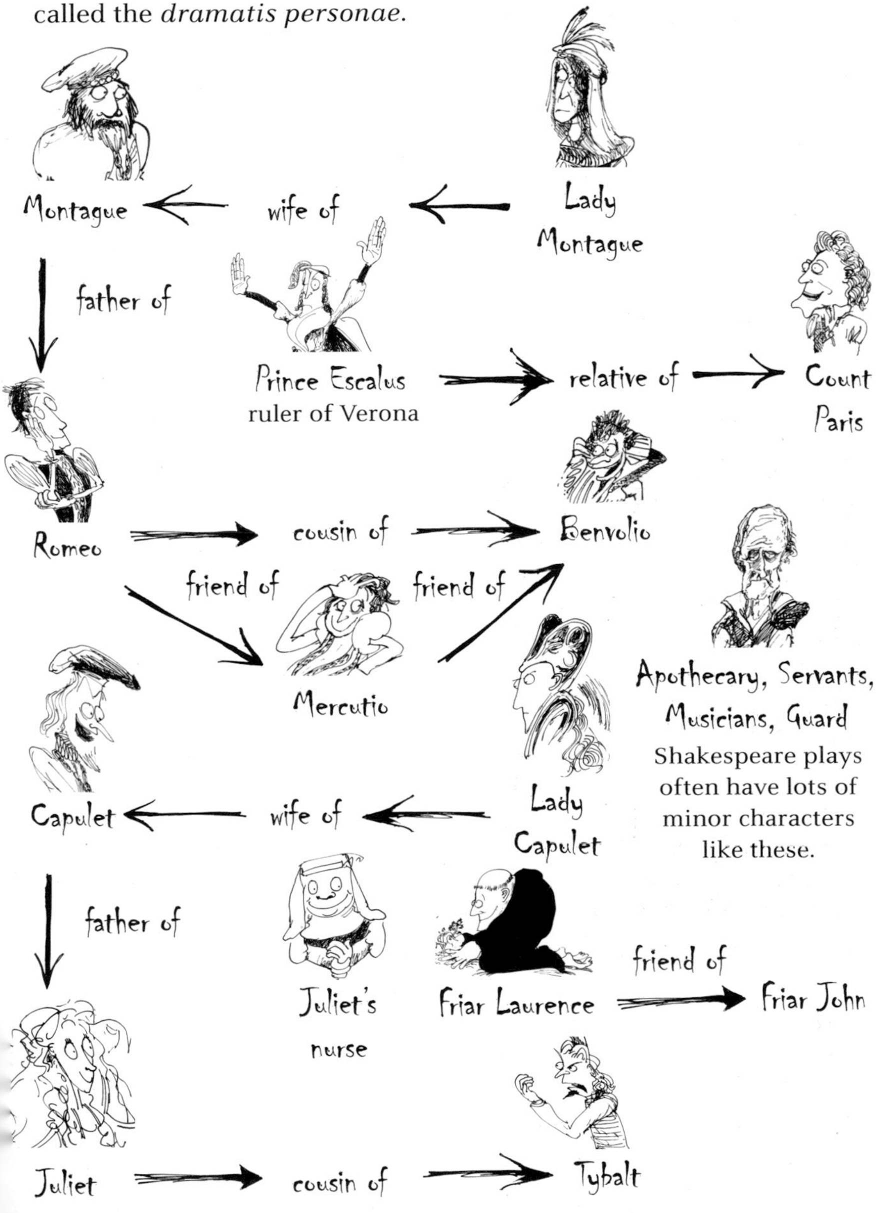

Montague ← wife of ← Lady Montague

Montague — father of → Romeo

Prince Escalus ruler of Verona — relative of → Count Paris

Romeo — cousin of → Benvolio

Romeo — friend of → Mercutio

Mercutio — friend of → Benvolio

Capulet ← wife of ← Lady Capulet

Capulet — father of → Juliet

Apothecary, Servants, Musicians, Guard

Shakespeare plays often have lots of minor characters like these.

Juliet's nurse

Friar Laurence — friend of → Friar John

Juliet — cousin of → Tybalt

Chapter One

It was a hot afternoon in Verona, and two servants from the Capulet household were walking across the market square.

"If I see any of those Montague dogs, I'll draw my sword," said Sampson.

"Here they come now," said Gregory, as two Montague servants appeared. "But don't start a fight – the Prince said no fighting." So, as the Montague men passed by, Sampson merely scowled in their faces.

"What are you looking at?" demanded Abram, Montague's servant. "Do you want a duel?"

"Me? No, no," Sampson replied innocently. "But if you do, I'll win. My master is better than your master, and clearly has better servants."

"Capulet is no better than Montague," said Abram. "And you're certainly no better than me."

They both drew their daggers and squared up to each other. "Prove it then, Montague scum," Sampson challenged.

"Stop that!" It was Benvolio, Montague's nephew. He drew his own sword as he approached.

"You idiots," he said. "Put your knives away!"

"Pulling a blade on my servants, are you?" Benvolio turned and saw Tybalt Capulet, the nephew of Old Capulet.

"No – I'm trying to keep the peace," said Benvolio.

"Yeah, right," Tybalt sneered. "Montague coward. If you want to fight, fight me."

"I don't..." Benvolio began, but Tybalt drew his own sword, and he had to defend himself. Before long, the servants joined in, and they all brawled their way across the square. The Prince's guards arrived and pulled the young men apart.

As the dust settled, Old Capulet himself came along with his wife. Through the crowd, he spotted Montague, his arch-enemy. "Get me a sword," he growled. "There's Old Montague, the slimy toad. I'll teach him a lesson."

"A sword?" his wife mocked. "A pair of crutches, more like. Don't be silly dear, you're far too old to fight. And it's banned, in case you hadn't noticed."

"Montague, you good-for-nothing old loser!" Capulet shouted. "Wait till I get my hands on you!"

"Just you try it!" Montague yelled back. He stepped forward, but his own wife grabbed his arm. "For goodness' sake!" she whispered. "Shh – the Prince is here!"

"**RIGHT!**" roared Prince Escalus, and the crowd fell silent. "Drop your weapons, every single one of you. This is the third street brawl we've seen in a month and I'm sick of it. So listen carefully. If ANYONE from the Montague or Capulet houses gets involved in another fight, they will be put to death.

...IS THAT CLEAR?!"

If ever you disturb our streets again, Your lives shall pay the forfeit of the peace.

What does that mean!?
"Forfeit" means a penalty. The Prince says anyone disturbing the peace will pay with their lives as a penalty.

When the Prince had gone, Montague and his wife asked Benvolio what had happened, and he explained.

"Well, thank goodness Romeo wasn't here," said Lady Montague. "He hates Tybalt. Where is Romeo, anyway?"

"Wandering in the woods, moping and daydreaming as usual," said Benvolio.

"Oh dear," said Old Montague. "I do hope he's not in love again. We've asked him what's going on, but he won't tell us."

"Look, here he comes now," said Benvolio. "I'll talk to him, and see if I can find out what's wrong." So Romeo's parents set off home, and Benvolio went up to his cousin.

"Hi Romeo, how are you?" he asked cheerily.

"Terrible!" Romeo groaned. "Heartbroken! I'm head-over-heels in love, but she doesn't love me!"

"Who?" Benvolio sighed.

"Her name's Rosaline..." Romeo said dreamily. "She's so beautiful. I just know she's the one!"

Benvolio smiled. "Come on, Romeo, come and have some fun. There are lots of other pretty girls."

"You'll never distract me from my true love!" Romeo wailed.

"Well, I'll do my best," said Benvolio.

Just then, a servant came hurrying up to them. "Could you help me, sirs? My master has given me this list of people to invite to a party tonight. But my eyesight is hopeless! Can you read it for me?"

"Of course," said Romeo. "It says: Martino's family, Anselm's family, Mrs. Utruvio, Lucio, Helena, Rosaline and Livia." Romeo gasped. "Where is this party?" he asked.

If you be not of the house of Montagues, I pray come and crush a cup of wine.

What does that mean!?
"I pray" means please, and "crush" means to drink or slurp.

"Why, at my master Capulet's house," said the man. "I'm sure you can come along too, if you like. As long as you're not Montagues, that is. Ha ha!"

"Well, it's a good job his eyesight's so bad," said Benvolio, once the man had gone. "Romeo, let's go! We can wear a disguise – no one will know it's us. You can show me this Rosaline, and I'll show you a dozen other girls who are prettier! It'll be fun! Come on, let's tell Mercutio. He'll want to come too." So they headed off to find their friend.

Upstairs in Capulet's house, his daughter Juliet was getting ready. Her nursemaid fussed around her, picking out ballgowns for her to try on.

"Juliet!" Lady Capulet came in.

"What is it?" asked Juliet, sitting down on the bed among the dresses.

"My darling," her mother began.
"As you know, you're growing up fast these days..."

"Isn't she just!?" cried the nurse. "Why, I remember when she was tiny, toddling to and fro! And now she's a young lady!
She'll be married before we know it!"

"That's exactly why I'm here," said Lady Capulet. "Juliet – how do you feel about getting married?"

"Mum!" gasped Juliet. "I'm only thirteen!"

"Nearly fourteen," said her mother. "Plenty of girls your age get married in Verona. And the fact is, Count Paris has asked for your hand in marriage, and we think he'd be perfect."

"Count Paris!" squealed the nurse. "Why Juliet, my poppet! He's tall, he's rich, he's handsome – you couldn't wish for more!"

"Paris will be here this evening," Lady Capulet went on. "I'd like you to dance with him and chat to him, and see if you like him. You will, of course. Now get dressed – the party is about to start."

"Married?" Juliet whispered, as the nurse buttoned up her best pink dress. She couldn't even imagine it.

The party was in full swing when Romeo, Benvolio and Mercutio arrived, wearing party masks as a disguise.
The ballroom was lit with candles, servants with silver platters moved among the finely dressed guests, and a band was playing on a stage.

14

Well, think of marriage now. Younger than you, Here in Verona, ladies of esteem, Are made already mothers.

What does that mean!?

Lady Capulet says that some girls in Verona, "of esteem", or from well-respected families, are married and even have children by Juliet's age

15

"Come on," Mercutio called. "Let's hit the dance floor and meet some girls!"

But Romeo looked worried. "I'm starting to think this wasn't a good idea," he said. "I've been having a dream that something bad might happen. Maybe it's this. We shouldn't be here."

"You and your dreams," teased Mercutio. "They're just silly bits of fluff, floating around in your brain. Stop thinking, Romeo – start dancing!" But Romeo refused. He would only sit and watch.

And as he watched, he suddenly saw the most enchanting, heart-stoppingly pretty girl he had ever laid eyes on. It was not Rosaline. Rosaline was forgotten at once.

This girl had honey-coloured hair, and eyes that sparkled with mischief and fun. She wore a pale pink party dress, and she was dancing politely with a man Romeo recognised – Count Paris.

He burned with jealousy as Paris, just for a moment, touched her arm.

"Who is that girl?" he asked a servant who was clearing up some dishes.

"Which one, sir?"

"The beautiful one, with the pink dress! That one!" But the servant couldn't tell which girl he meant.

What Romeo didn't know was that Tybalt was standing nearby. He knew he had heard the masked stranger's voice before. Romeo Montague! Tybalt rushed off to find Old Capulet.

"Uncle," he said, "there's a Montague here. Romeo Montague. He's sneaked into our party, and I bet his friends have too. I'll fetch my sword, and get rid of them."

"No, Tybalt," said Old Capulet. "Remember what the Prince said."

"But Uncle! The Montagues are our enemies!"

"Goodness knows I hate Old Montague," Capulet said. "But his son has caused me no harm. He's here now, and that means he's my guest. Calm down, Tybalt, and leave it."

Tybalt was furious. "I'll get that Romeo Montague," he swore. "As soon as I get a chance."

Show a fair presence and put
off these frowns,
An ill-beseeming semblance for a feast.

The dance ended, and Romeo saw the girl heading
for a doorway. He followed her, and found her
standing alone just outside the ballroom.

"My lady," Romeo began. He reached out and took
her hand, and she blushed. "I'm sorry," Romeo
said. "My hand isn't worthy to touch yours.
I could kiss you instead, if you like."

"I couldn't possibly agree to that. It wouldn't
be ladylike," the girl smiled.

19

"But if I kiss you, will you mind?"

"I'm not going anywhere," said Juliet.

So Romeo kissed her, and she kissed him back. She had no idea who this boy was, but she felt very differently about kissing him than she did about dancing with stuffy old Count Paris.

"Sweetie-pie, where are you?" Juliet's nurse came bustling out of the ballroom. "Your parents want you, poppet," she said, and Juliet hurried away.

"Who are her parents?" Romeo asked the nurse.

"Why, Lord and Lady Capulet, of course, and she's my little Juliet, my sweetie-pie!" said the nurse.

"Juliet Capulet?" said Romeo. "She's a Capulet?" The news felt like a knife blade in his heart. Now he was truly in love – really and truly, more than ever before. But the girl he loved was the daughter of his father's worst enemy!

"There you are, Romeo!" Mercutio and Benvolio appeared. "The party's winding down," said Benvolio. "It's time to go".

Romeo was staring into space, struck dumb with love and heartbreak – as he always was. So Mercutio and Benvolio simply grabbed him and dragged him away.

The next moment, Juliet came hurrying back. "Where's he gone!?" she asked the nurse. "Where's that boy?"

"You can forget about him, darling," the nurse said. She had heard Romeo's friends say his name.

"But why? Who is he?"

"That's Romeo, sweetheart. Romeo Montague. I don't think your parents will think he's a suitable husband, now, will they? Come on, let's go and say goodnight to Count Paris. It's almost bedtime."

Chapter Two

As soon as the friends had made their way out through the Capulet gates, Romeo vanished again. The others called for him, and searched for him in the darkness, but he was nowhere to be found.

"He's probably wandered off to mope and moan in the moonlight," Mercutio said. "He'll be fine." So they went home to bed.

In fact, Romeo had climbed over the wall into the Capulets' orchard garden. He hid among the apple trees until he saw a light in one of the bedrooms. Seconds later, Juliet came onto the balcony.

"It's her!" he gasped. "Her beauty shines like the Sun – brighter even than the moonlight!" Juliet sighed, and he crept closer to hear her.

Oh Romeo, Romeo, wherefore art thou Romeo? Deny thy father and refuse thy name.

What does that mean!?
Juliet asks why ("wherefore") the boy she loves must have the name of Montague, wishing he would deny or reject it.

"Oh Romeo, Romeo!" she called, not knowing he was there. "Why must you be a Montague? If only you could change your name and leave your family, we could be together. What's in a name, after all? A rose with a different name would smell the same!"

"I'd do it gladly, my lady," Romeo called up.

"Who's there!?" Juliet gasped. "Romeo? Is that you?"

"Well, you don't like that name, so I'd happily change it. But yes, it's me."

"Romeo! What are you doing in the garden? How did you get in? The guards will kill you!"

"I had to see you, Juliet. I love you. And if you love me too, I'll marry you. Just say the word."

"You've already heard me say I do," Juliet said, "but our parents would never agree. If we marry, it must be in secret – and soon. Otherwise, they'll make me marry Paris, and it will be too late."

"I can arrange it," said Romeo bravely. "Send a servant to meet me in the square tomorrow, at nine in the morning. I will give them a message for you. We will be married, Juliet."

From inside the house, Juliet's nurse was calling her. "I must go," she said. "Goodnight, Romeo! Parting is such sweet sorrow!"

"Goodnight, Juliet!" Romeo watched as she went in and closed the door. Then, with his heart pounding, he climbed back over the wall, and ran not home, but to the one person who could help him – the old monk, Friar Laurence.

It was dawn by the time Romeo reached Friar Laurence's cottage, and the Friar was awake, tending his herb garden. He always listened to Romeo's problems, and helped him when he could. He could also carry out weddings.

What does that mean!?
"Didst" means "did" and "thou" means "you", the Friar is amazed at how quickly Romeo has forsaken, or abandoned, his love for Rosaline.

"What can I do for you this morning, Romeo?" he asked calmly, as Romeo hurtled through his garden gate. "You look as if you haven't even been to bed!"

"Please help me, Friar," said Romeo. "I'm in love – with Juliet Capulet. I want to marry her."

"Juliet who?" chuckled the Friar. "What about Rosaline? I thought you were in love with her!"

So Romeo told him about the Capulet party, and how he had met Juliet and fallen in love – and had sworn he would marry her before her parents promised her to anyone else.

"My goodness, all those tears you wasted on Rosaline, when you didn't love her at all!" smiled the Friar.

"I didn't," Romeo agreed. "This is true love. And Juliet loves me too. Please, please help us."

The Friar could see that Romeo's heart was true, and he was sorry for him. But more than that, he thought that maybe, just maybe, the young couple's love could end the fighting between their families.

"Two o'clock today," he said. "Make sure you are both here, and you will be married. I will break the news to your parents when the time is right."

Romeo still hadn't had any sleep, but he could not go home yet. It was already past nine o'clock in the morning, the time he had told Juliet he would be in the market square to pass on a message.

Mercutio and Benvolio were waiting for him. "Romeo, what on Earth have you been up to?" Mercutio greeted him. "You look as pale and tired as a dried fish! And don't think we didn't notice you sneaking off last night. Where did you go?"

"I had important business to attend to," said Romeo, smiling. "Really important."

"I see!" said Mercutio. "To do with girls, perhaps?"

"Maybe," said Romeo. "You'll find out."

"Well, there's someone else who wants to do business with you – Tybalt," said Benvolio. "Watch out for him, Romeo – he's on the warpath."

But at that moment, Romeo spotted Juliet's nurse. "I must talk to this lady," he told his friends. "Will you go to my house, and tell my father I will be home soon? I'll meet you there for lunch."

"Whatever you say, lover boy!" Mercutio teased, and off they went.

Seeing Romeo was alone, the nurse came up to him, looking around carefully before she spoke.

"Now listen to me, my young sir. My Juliet has told me everything, and I swear I can keep a secret. But you must promise me, Romeo, that you love her. That you'll do right by her, and marry her, and stay with her always. Because I just want my girl to be happy, and that's the only reason I'm helping you – because she wants to be with you, and not that rich, handsome Count Paris. Do you hear me, Romeo?"

"Yes," said Romeo seriously. "You have my word, I love her, and will never leave her."

"Good," said the nurse. "Then tell me the plan."

Juliet watched from her balcony until she saw her nurse hurrying home. She ran to meet her.

"What happened? What did he say!?"

"Goodness, give me a moment, sweetie-pie! Oh, how my old bones ache. What a walk I've had!"

"Tell me, nurse, tell me what he said!"

"Can you visit old Friar Laurence this afternoon?"

"Yes, of course," said Juliet.

"Then go, my darling, at two o'clock. You'll find a husband waiting for you there."

"Nurse!" Juliet hugged her tight, and the nurse wiped away a tear. "I must have my lunch now," she sniffed. "Go on, my darling. Off you go."

Then hie you hence to Friar Laurence's cell. There stays a husband to make you a wife.

What does that mean!?
The nurse tells Juliet to hurry over to the Friar's "cell", or hut, where Romeo "stays" or waits for her.

At Friar Laurence's cottage, the Friar was trying to give Romeo a few words of advice. "A marriage is for ever, Romeo," he said. "The passion you feel now is like a firework, that flashes brightly, and burns out. But true love is a different story."

As Romeo nodded seriously, the cottage door burst open, and Juliet rushed in, flinging herself into his arms. They covered each other's faces with kisses, and gazed into each other's eyes.

"OK," said Friar Laurence. "Come on, you two. Let's get this wedding under way."

Chapter Three

That afternoon, Benvolio and Mercutio were back in the market square, waiting for Romeo – again.

"Phew, it's hot!" said Benvolio. "And the Capulets are around. Maybe we should go somewhere else."

"I'll wait where I like," said Mercutio. "It takes two sides to fight. If we don't fight, there'll be no fight."

"Who's talking about fighting?" They turned and saw Tybalt, his hand on the handle of his sword.

"No one," said Mercutio. "We have no quarrel with you, Tybalt. Now run along, there's a good boy."

"Well I have a quarrel with you," Tybalt snarled. "You're Romeo's friends, and he's my enemy."

"I'm not your enemy." It was Romeo. Tybalt turned to face him, scowling in the bright sunlight. "You and I have every reason to be friends, Tybalt," Romeo went on. "And soon you'll find out why."

"You think you can get away with sneaking into my uncle's house with a few smarmy words?" Tybalt sneered. "You're cowards, all of you. Draw your sword, and fight."

"I won't fight," said Romeo. But Mercutio had stood up angrily. "Watch how you speak to my friends," he said. "Or you'll have me to answer to."

"Fair enough, I'll fight you," Tybalt replied, and in the next second, both their swords were drawn.

"No, Mercutio!" Romeo shouted, and tried to force his way in between them. But Tybalt reached past him and stabbed Mercutio in the chest.

"It's just a scratch," Mercutio laughed. But suddenly he slumped to his knees. "I can't breathe," he said in a strangled voice. "Get a doctor. Curse you both, Montagues and Capulets. Curse you all."

Romeo watched in horror as Mercutio keeled forwards onto the paving stones, then lay still.

I am hurt.
A plague o' both your houses!
I am sped.

What does that mean!?
Mercutio curses both houses - of Montague and Capulet - wishing a plague or disease on them.
"I am sped" means "I'm done for".

"You've killed him," said Romeo, trembling with anger. "Tybalt, you murdering, evil..."

Romeo grabbed Mercutio's sword, and before anyone could stop him he charged at Tybalt. Tybalt barely had time to turn around before Romeo plunged the blade through his stomach.

Benvolio was horrified. "Romeo, what have you done!?" he cried, as Tybalt choked and spluttered on the ground, desperately drawing his last few breaths. "Romeo, run, get away! The Prince will come, and you'll be put to death! Run!"

So Romeo ran to the safest place he knew – Friar Laurence's house.

The Prince's guards soon arrived, followed by the Prince himself. Benvolio told him everything. "But Romeo was provoked," he pleaded. "Tybalt had just killed our friend. Tybalt started it."

"He would say that, wouldn't he?" shouted a Capulet from the crowd. "He's a Montague."

"Well, Tybalt would have been executed anyway, for killing Mercutio," a Montague voice taunted back. "Romeo just did the Prince's job for him!"

"That's enough," said Prince Escalus, calmly. "Romeo was provoked, and so I won't sentence him to death. But I hereby exile him. He must leave the city of Verona, and not be seen here again."

Meanwhile, Juliet was waiting in her room, wishing with all her heart that night would come. She had kissed her new husband goodbye, and made him promise that as soon as it was dark, he would sneak back into the Capulets' orchard, climb up to her balcony, and spend the night with her in secret.

But when the nurse came bursting into the room, with a distraught look on her face, Juliet knew something was very wrong.

"Oh my sweetheart! My pet! He's dead, my darling! He's dead, he's dead, he's dead!"

"Who is? Who's dead? Not Romeo!?" Juliet's hands flew to her mouth.

"No, not Romeo – Tybalt! Your dear cousin Tybalt is dead!"

"Tybalt!?" Juliet sat down on the bed in shock, but also flooded with relief. Romeo was not dead.

"But why, what happened? Was there a fight?"

"A fight, yes, and Romeo killed Tybalt! Romeo is banished! He must leave, never to return!"

"Romeo? Romeo!?" Juliet burst into tears. "How could he!? He's only just married me! He was going to come and see me here, tonight!"

"Hush, my love," said her nurse, comforting her. "It wasn't Romeo's fault. Well, not really. Men are all the same, of course, hot-headed show-offs. But it was Tybalt that started the fight.

Listen – I know where Romeo is. He's hiding at the Friar's house. He must leave Verona by dawn tomorrow... but it's only right that he should say goodbye. I'll go there, and tell him to come to you tonight."

"Give him my ring," said Juliet, "to show him I still love him."

At the Friar's cottage, Romeo was collapsed in a heap on the floor, sobbing.

"Come on, Romeo," the Friar consoled him. "It's not the end of the world. The Prince could have executed you. He's shown great mercy."

"I might as well be dead, as be away from Juliet!" Romeo wailed.

There was a knock at the door. "It's me," called the nurse.
"Let me in – I have a message from Juliet!"

They both stood shaking their heads at Romeo's self-pitying
groaning. "Goodness me, young sir," the nurse scolded. "Be a
man, for poor Juliet's sake. She's waiting for you now,
and you can still visit her, if you're sure to leave by
dawn. Look, she gave me this ring for you, as a sign
of her love."

What does that mean!?

Romeo says to
be outside
("without") the
city of Verona
is torture and
"purgatory", a
state of pain and
misery, while
being in Verona
and close to
Juliet is heaven.

"Romeo, can't you see how lucky you are?" said the Friar in exasperation. "You are newly married, and in love. Tybalt wanted to kill you, but he failed. And the Prince has spared you. Go to Juliet tonight. Then, before dawn, flee to Mantua, which is not far away. When all this has died down, I'll explain everything to the Prince, and your parents. With any luck, you'll be pardoned, and you and Juliet can live happily ever after."

"It's getting dark," the nurse said. "Wipe your eyes, darling – go to her now. Your secret's safe with us."

The Capulet household was deep in mourning for Tybalt, and Old Capulet was very worried about his daughter. Tybalt was her cousin, but they had never been close. Why did she seem so devastated?

When Count Paris came to pay his respects, he asked Capulet politely if Juliet would marry him.

"I know a wedding is not something we can think about just now, at such a sad time," he said. "But my offer is still there."

Capulet thought about it for a moment. "Wait," he said, "I think it might be a good time, after all. Juliet has taken all this very badly. Maybe she needs something to take her mind off it. I agree to the wedding, my friend. In fact, I think it should take place as soon as possible. On Thursday."

"Thursday!?"

Juliet could not believe her ears.

Minutes earlier, she had been standing on her balcony, kissing her beloved Romeo goodbye as the sun rose. He had to go – it was already dawn – but every time he pulled away, he came back to kiss her again, and again... until the nurse ran in to warn them that Lady Capulet was on her way to see Juliet at that very moment.

"Go, Romeo! Goodbye! Goodbye!" Juliet whispered as he climbed quickly over the balcony wall, and jumped down into the garden. A moment later, he had disappeared among the apple trees.

And then her mother had come in, and told her the wonderful, exciting news – that she was going to marry Count Paris on Thursday.

"NO," said Juliet firmly. "I won't."

"You won't?" gasped her mother. "It's not up to you who you marry, Juliet – it's up to your father!"

Then Old Capulet came in. "What's this I hear? No? *No?* You ungrateful child. The wealthiest, most handsome man in Verona offers to marry you, and you say no!?"

"Please," Juliet begged him, falling to her knees. "Please don't make me marry him."

What does that mean!?
Capulet calls Juliet a "baggage" meaning an immoral woman, and says if she doesn't obey him, he will disown her. "Thee" means you.

"Your lordship..." the nurse began.
"If she doesn't love the Count..."

"Silence! You'll do as you're told, young lady!"
her father shouted. "You'll get yourself to that
church on Thursday, or I'll drag you there! No, indeed!"

Juliet's parents left her crying on her bed, while her nurse
hugged her.

"I can't marry Paris," she sobbed. "I can't!"

"Oh my pet. Oh, sweetheart," the nurse said. "There's nothing
for it, darling. You'll have to go through with the wedding, or
else your father will suspect. We must try and make the best
of it."

Juliet was horrified. Would no one help her? At last she said,
"Maybe you're right. I'll go and see Friar Laurence. Please tell
my parents I'm asking his advice, to help me to prepare for
married life."

But Juliet really planned to beg the Friar to help her escape.
And if he couldn't, she would rather die.

Chapter Four

As Juliet strode towards Friar Laurence's cottage, she had
no idea that Paris was already there. He had gone to tell Friar
Laurence about his sudden wedding plans.

"On Thursday? And you don't even know how Juliet feels
about it?" Friar Laurence asked.

"Her father thinks it best, as she's so upset about Tybalt," Paris explained.

"Thursday, indeed," muttered the Friar. Then, through the window, he saw Juliet at his garden gate. A second later, she opened the door.

"Juliet!" said Paris in surprise. "How lovely to see you. My – erm, dearest wife-to-be."

"Hello, Paris," said Juliet. "I don't think you can count on that yet. Not until Thursday, anyway. I'd like to see the Friar in private, if you don't mind."

"Oh – er, sorry, yes of course." Paris leaned over and gave Juliet an awkward kiss on the cheek. "Until Thursday."

The moment the door closed behind him, Juliet broke down in tears. "Oh Friar!" she howled. "I'm beyond help now! How can I get out of this mess?"

"I'm so sorry, Juliet," the Friar said sadly. "I can't see a way out of it."

"If you can't help me," said Juliet, "I'll take the only way out I can." She showed the Friar that she had a dagger hidden in her cloak.

"Juliet, no, don't think of that!" Friar Laurence gasped. "My dear, if you're that desperate, there is something we could try." He took a small bottle from a cupboard.

"This is a very strong medicine, made from the herbs in my garden," the Friar said. "Tomorrow night, when you are alone, drink it – all of it. It will send you into a deep sleep – so deep that you will seem to be dead. Your family will take your body to the Capulet vault*. Meanwhile, I will write to Romeo with a plan. He can return to Verona under cover of darkness, wake you up and rescue you. Then I will help you both escape to Mantua."

*A vault is an underground stone cellar where bodies are laid to rest.

No warmth, no breath shall testify thou livest, The roses in thy lips and cheeks shall fade...

48

What does that mean!?
The Friar describes how Juliet
will seem to have no warmth or
breath to prove she's alive, and
the "roses" or pink colour in her
face will disappear.

When Juliet got home, she went to see her father and told him she was sorry for her disobedience. She said she would marry Paris, and spent the next day pretending to be interested in which dress to wear. Her father was delighted that Juliet had finally seen sense.

But all the time, the precious bottle was hidden safely under her bed.

On Wednesday night, she said she wanted to go to bed early. Then, with the door tightly shut, she took out the bottle, uncorked it, and drank it down.

49

When dawn broke, old Capulet was already up. He was quite
excited about the wedding. He ordered his servants here and
there, telling them to get logs ready for the fireplaces and bake
meat and pastries for the wedding feast.

"Dear me," Juliet's nurse muttered as she hurried by.
"What an old housewife!"

"Ah, Nurse," called Capulet. "Are you going to wake up Juliet?
Hurry – she has to get ready!"

The nurse opened Juliet's door. "Juliet! Juliet? Come on,
sleepyhead! Wake up! It's your wedding day, darling!"

Juliet didn't move. The nurse went over and shook her. "Juliet, poppet? Still sound asleep?" But as she brushed Juliet's hair off her face, she realised that her skin was icy cold.

The nurse's scream brought everyone running to the bedroom. The whole house was plunged into chaos as the news spread that Juliet was dead. Musicians were sent home, and the wedding feast was left half-prepared in the kitchens. And poor Count Paris arrived in the middle of the commotion, only to be told his bride-to-be had died in the night.

Why, lamb, why, lady, fie! You slug-abed! Why, love, I say! Madam! Sweetheart! What, not a word?

What does that mean!?
The nurse repeatedly calls Juliet, saying "fie!", an expression of disapproval, and "slug-abed" meaning a lazy person.

Chapter Five

Meanwhile, in Mantua, Romeo was miserable, and missing Juliet with all his heart. But when he woke up on Thursday morning, he felt a little better. He had had a dream about Juliet, and he hoped that meant he might see her soon.

He heard someone running up the stairs and banging on his door. It was Balthasar, the only Montague servant he had entrusted with his secret. "Balthasar!" Romeo jumped up eagerly. "Is there news from Verona?"

Yes, sir, but terrible news!" Balthasar panted. "Juliet is dead, Romeo – found dead this morning."

Romeo felt his blood turn to ice. He took a step back and sat down heavily on his bed.

Well, Juliet, I will lie with thee tonight.

"Balthasar... find me a horse, and a pen and paper. I'm coming back to Verona, and I will give you a letter to take to my father."

"At once, sir!" Balthasar ran off.

"Well, Juliet, I will see you tonight," he said sadly. "For if you are dead, I want to die too – so I have nothing to fear in Verona. All I want is to lie by your side. And I know someone who can help me."

Down a tiny dark side street in Mantua stood an old shop. Its dusty wooden shelves were filled with green glass jars of herbs, dried flowers and mysterious dark liquids. From the rafters hung an ancient stuffed crocodile, and behind the counter lurked a wizened, bony old man.

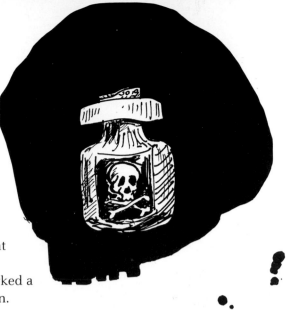

The door creaked as Romeo came in. "Apothecary?" he called quietly into the gloom.

"Here, young man."

"I need poison," said Romeo. "A poison strong enough to kill any man, and fast."

"I have it," the apothecary said. "But such poison is against the law in Mantua. I couldn't sell it to you."

"You are a poor old man," said Romeo, looking into his eyes, "and I have forty gold coins."

The old man took Romeo's bag of coins, and silently handed him a tiny bottle.

That evening, Friar Laurence was watering his herb garden, and worrying to himself. He had sent his friend Friar John to take the letter to Romeo. It explained exactly what Juliet had done and how Romeo must rescue her. But John should be back by now. Where was he?

"Laurence!" Friar John was at his gate.

"Oh, thank goodness. Did Romeo get the letter?"

"I'm so sorry, but no. I was visiting the sick this morning, and the guards told me I couldn't leave Verona, in case I spread disease. I never made it to Mantua. Here's the letter – I couldn't deliver it."

"Oh, no," said the Friar. He dropped his watering can and set off for the Capulet vault at once. He would have to rescue Juliet himself, and hide her at his house. If he didn't act fast, she might end up being buried! "Oh my goodness, I do hope she's alright!" the Friar fretted as he headed for the vault at top speed.

Juliet lay as cold and still as a stone in a tomb in the vault. But she was not alone. Count Paris had secretly come to pay his last respects to her, leaving his servant outside to keep watch.

The sad count stood over the girl who had never loved him, gently scattering some flower petals over her. "Sleep well, Juliet," he said. Then his servant whistled to signal that someone was coming. Paris hid in the shadows.

The letter was not nice, but full of charge. And dear import!

What does that mean!?
Friar Laurence explains his letter was not "nice", meaning polite or trivial, but contained precious and important news.

It was Romeo. Paris watched him walk quietly across the vault to Juliet's body, lean over, and kiss her. He was furious.

"What are you doing here, vile Montague murderer?" he demanded, approaching Romeo with his dagger drawn. "You're banned from Verona! You killed Tybalt, and that's why poor Juliet died – of grief, at what you did."

"Don't fight me, Paris," Romeo replied. "I am here to die myself. I have nothing to lose, so I'd stay out of my way if I were you."

"Never. I'll defend poor Juliet's honour," Paris blustered. "Stand and fight!" So Romeo drew his dagger too, and as Paris came towards him, he stabbed him in the throat.

"Help! I am slain!" Paris gurgled, sending his servant running for the guards.

Romeo knew he had very little time. He turned back to his beloved Juliet, and kissed her again. "How can she still look so beautiful?" he whispered. "It's as if she's only sleeping! Even death cannot hide your beauty, Juliet."

He took the apothecary's bottle from his pocket, and opened it. "Juliet, I'll come to join you," he said, and kissed her again. Then he tipped up the bottle, drank the poison, and fell down beside her.

For a moment, there was silence. Then the sound of frantic footsteps echoed around the vault, as Friar Laurence rushed in.

"Juliet, wake up!" he called. Then he saw the bodies of Romeo and Paris, lying in the shadows nearby. "Oh my goodness! Oh, no, oh, my dear!"

"Friar Laurence?" Juliet was stirring awake. "Oh Friar, I am alive! It worked! Where is Romeo?"

"Oh my dear girl. Oh, all is lost! Juliet, let me take you to safety. Don't look around you. Come, now!"

But Juliet did look around her. She saw Paris. She saw Romeo, and the bottle in his hand. "Romeo?"

"Juliet, please. The Prince's men will come soon."

"Then leave, Friar, before they come. They must not catch you here," said Juliet calmly. The poor Friar had no choice. He hurried back outside, only to run straight into the guards.

Juliet got up from her resting place, and knelt down beside Romeo. She took the bottle from his hand. "What, you've left none for me?" she said. "I'll kiss you – maybe some poison will be left on your lips." She kissed him. "I love you, Romeo. Let me die, and we'll be together at last."

She reached for the dagger Romeo had used to kill Paris. "Just to make sure," Juliet said, and she forced the blade deep into her own heart. The guards arrived too late. The young lovers lay dead, side by side.

As soon as Prince Escalus was told, he called the

Montague and Capulet families to the vault. There he ordered Friar Laurence to explain exactly what had been going on. As the Friar told the whole story, dabbing at his tears, Old Montague, Romeo's father, came forward. "Your Highness, all the Friar says is true. Romeo wrote me a letter before he died, which I have only just received." He handed the letter to the Prince, who read it carefully.

"Poor Romeo and Juliet," he said. "Their chance of happiness is lost. And all because your families held such hatred. Well, no more. They will be buried together, and unite your families in death."

"Montague." Old Capulet was holding out his hand. "I'm sorry. Let us be friends, and live in peace." And the two old men shook hands, then hugged each other in their grief.

"Let us learn from this," said the Prince. "And make sure it never happens again. We will always remember the sad tale of Juliet, and her Romeo."

For never was a story of more woe
Than this of Juliet, and her Romeo.

61

ROMEO AND JULIET
AT A GLANCE

Though *Romeo and Juliet* is a tragedy, with a disastrous, violent ending, it is one of the most popular plays that Shakespeare wrote. It's also one of the most often performed – both in Shakespeare's own time, and ever since.

Romeo and Juliet as a play

The story in this book is told in prose, but Shakespeare wrote the original *Romeo and Juliet* as a play. Instead of descriptions and explanations, it's almost all made up of dialogue, or words spoken by the characters. There are also stage directions, or instructions for the actors to follow.

Here you can see part of *Romeo and Juliet*, as Shakespeare wrote it, including the stage directions. It's the scene where Romeo kills Tybalt:

TYBALT: Thou wretched boy, that didst consort him here,
Shalt with him hence.
ROMEO: This shall determine that.
They fight. Tybalt falls.

BENVOLIO: Romeo, away, be gone.
The citizens are up, and Tybalt slain!
Stand not amaz'd. The Prince will doom thee death
If thou art taken. Hence, be gone, away!
ROMEO: Oh, I am fortune's fool.
BENVOLIO: Why dost thou stay?

Stage directions

Exit Romeo.

FACT FILE:
FULL TITLE: The Most Excellent and Lamentable
Tragedy of Romeo and Juliet
DATE WRITTEN: around 1594-5
LENGTH: 3,058 lines

Acts and scenes

Shakespeare broke all his plays up into five main sections or acts, and smaller sections called scenes, each set in a different place. These help to give a play structure, jumping from one place to another to build up the story. They also make it easier for actors to learn their lines in handy chunks.

THE FIVE ACTS OF *ROMEO AND JULIET*

ACT 1 **(5 scenes)**
Act 1 introduces the Montague-Capulet feud, and Romeo and Juliet meet and fall in love at the Capulet party.

ACT 2 **(6 scenes)**
Romeo and Juliet declare their love and marry in secret.

ACT 3 **(5 scenes)**
Romeo kills Tybalt in a fight and is banished from Verona, while Juliet is told she must marry Paris.

ACT 4 **(5 scenes)**
With Friar Laurence's help, Juliet takes a potion to make her seem dead, so Romeo can rescue her.

ACT 5 **(3 scenes)**
The plan goes wrong and Romeo and Juliet kill themselves, each believing the other to be dead.

THE STORY OF
ROMEO AND JULIET

For most of his plays, Shakespeare did not come up with
a new plot. Instead, he based his plays on real people and their
lives, or borrowed stories from myths, legends, folktales and
old books. He would often take several of these and
weave them together to make a more complex play.

A well-known tale

Tales of forbidden love going disastrously wrong date
back to ancient times, and have always been popular.
Shakespeare based *Romeo and Juliet* on an Italian version
of the theme. The story had been told and retold by several
different Italian authors in the 1400s and 1500s, each of
them adding more details and characters of their own.

By the time Shakespeare decided to
rework the story into a play in the
1590s, it was already very detailed
and well-known. He didn't have to
come up with many new characters
or details – it was all there already.

Were Romeo and Juliet real?

History books show there were two rival families
living in Verona sometime around the 1300s, who
were called the Montecchi and the Cappelletti. It's
likely that this is the source of the names "Montague"
and "Capulet". However, no one knows if Romeo
and Juliet themselves ever really existed,
or if the forbidden love story is true.

64

The city of Verona

Verona, the town where *Romeo and Juliet* is set, is a real place in Italy. The play describes its city walls and some of its buildings. This picture shows what it was like around Shakespeare's time:

That's not my balcony!

Fun Fact!

Today in Verona you can visit "Juliet's house" and see "Juliet's balcony" - but there's no evidence it really was her house. The balcony was actually added in the 1930s to attract tourists!

SHAKESPEARE AND
ROMEO AND JULIET

Why did Shakespeare write *Romeo and Juliet*? The main reason was probably simply because he knew it would be a hit. Shakespeare wrote plays to be performed, and they had to attract paying audiences.

Shakespeare at work

William Shakespeare was born in the quiet town of Stratford-upon-Avon, England, but moved to London to become an actor and playwright. We don't know exactly when he arrived, but he is thought to have been in London by 1592, and in 1594 he joined a new theatre company, the Chamberlain's Men.

Pulling in the crowds

Romeo and Juliet was written around this time, and would have been one of the first performances the new company put on. Shakespeare had already written a few plays, but he was not very experienced. The fact that he chose such a well-known and ready-made story reflects this. It was guaranteed to draw crowds, just as a well-known pantomime or a film based on a bestselling book do today.

They'll love this bit!

Tragedy and comedy

Romeo and Juliet is a tragedy, but it's an unusual one for Shakespeare. Most of his tragedies, like *Macbeth*, *Hamlet* and *King Lear*, are about leaders who make serious mistakes or become corrupt, resulting in a disastrous downfall.

In *Romeo and Juliet*, the lead characters are young lovers, and we are on their side all the way through. Juliet, the main female character, is just as important as Romeo, and has almost as many lines and speeches as him. And there are plenty of funny scenes and comic characters like the nurse. In these ways, *Romeo and Juliet* has more in common with Shakespeare's comedies than his other tragedies.

STAGING *ROMEO AND JULIET*

London is full of theatres today, but in the 1590s, there weren't many. The Chamberlain's Men used two: The Theatre, built in 1576 by James Burbage, the company's founder, and another theatre nearby, called The Curtain. Plays were also put on in pub courtyards, or sometimes in royal palaces to entertain Queen Elizabeth I and her court.

In 1599, the Chamberlain's Men built another new theatre, the Globe, on the south bank of the River Thames, and *Romeo and Juliet* probably appeared here too.

Fun Fact!
Fake blood

Romeo and Juliet has quite a few gory stabbing scenes. To fake a stab wound, the actors would tie an animal's bladder filled with pig or sheep's blood under their armpit. The blade would stab this, making the blood burst out!

What were theatres like?

Theatres in Shakespeare's time were inspired by ancient Greek and Roman theatres, and were open-air. The stage was surrounded by a flat standing area, and around this was a ring-shaped, roofed building with three levels of seats.

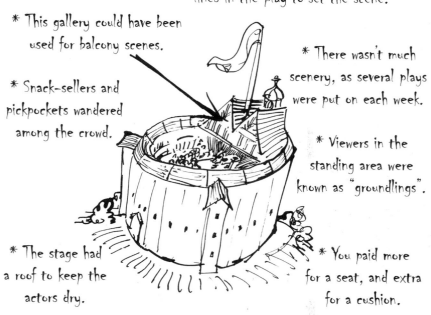

* Actors used costumes, props and the lines in the play to set the scene.

* This gallery could have been used for balcony scenes.

* Snack-sellers and pickpockets wandered among the crowd.

* There wasn't much scenery, as several plays were put on each week.

* Viewers in the standing area were known as "groundlings".

* The stage had a roof to keep the actors dry.

* You paid more for a seat, and extra for a cushion.

Who played who?

Shakespeare's company had a team of actors, including Shakespeare himself, who played the main roles. They were all male – there were no female actors at this time. So female parts, such as Juliet and the nurse, would have been played by boys. Robert Goffe, a young trainee actor, may have been the first to play Juliet, while the part of Romeo would have gone to Richard Burbage (James Burbage's son), the company's star actor.

ROMEO AND JULIET: THEMES AND SYMBOLS

When you read a Shakespeare play, you can often spot patterns, themes and images that are repeated all the way through. They help to hold the story together and make the important moments more memorable. Here are some of *Romeo and Juliet's* main themes and symbols:

Love

Of course, first and foremost, *Romeo and Juliet* is a love story. The passionate, romantic love between the two teenagers drives the action forward, and a lot of lines are devoted to expressing how much they love each other.

ROMEO:
What light through yonder window breaks?
It is the East, and Juliet is the Sun.

JULIET:
My bounty is as boundless as the sea,
My love as deep.

However, this isn't the only kind of love in the play. It also explores the love between Romeo and his friends, Benvolio and Mercutio – expressed through their endless teasing. And it takes a look at two older couples, the Capulets and the Montagues, who are married, but don't seem to care much about each other, or their children.

Perhaps the most powerful love in the story comes from two characters who are actually single – the Friar and the nurse. They love Romeo and Juliet like their own children, do all they can to help them, and are the most upset when things go wrong. The play makes you think about what "true love" is, and where it really comes from.

Pairs and opposites
The central theme of the play is a pair of two opposites – the children of two enemy families. This is echoed by many other pairs found in the play.

Benvolio and Tybalt are both cousins of the main characters – one kind, one hasty and violent. Benvolio's name means "good will" and Tybalt's means "bold".

Capulet and Montague themselves, their houses and servants, form more opposing pairs in the play.

The nurse and the Friar team up to help Romeo and Juliet, like a pair of loving parents. But they are opposites too – the nurse is clucky and gossipy, the Friar a serious, holy man.

Light and dark
The theme of opposites is reflected in repeated imagery of light and darkness. Romeo and Juliet describe each other as glowing sunlight, stars, lanterns or lightning, and the Friar compares their love to a burning firework – contrasting with the dark night-time settings where they meet and spend time together. As the play nears its end, darkness takes over, with the gloomy apothecary's shop, and the final darkness of the Capulet burial vault.

DEADLY POISON

One of the most evocative scenes in *Romeo and Juliet* is
Romeo's visit to the old apothecary – a kind of traditional
chemist and medicine-maker. The apothecary sells him a
poison guaranteed to kill him quickly, even though he says
this is against Mantuan law. What would the poison have
been, and did scenes like this happen in real life?

Poison through history

Poison has been used to kill people since ancient times.
Greek, Roman, Egyptian and ancient Indian societies knew of
plant poisons such as hemlock and wolfsbane, and poisonous
minerals such as arsenic, as well as sometimes using deadly
snake venom. (Egyptian queen Cleopatra was said to have
killed herself by allowing a cobra to bite her, and this appears
in another Shakespeare play, *Antony and Cleopatra*.)

In the Medieval and Renaissance eras, including
Shakespeare's time, Italy was famous for its apothecaries
and their poison recipes. People often
used poison as a sneaky way to
get rid of enemies, political
opponents, and even
unwanted husbands.

Deadly recipe

The apothecary doesn't say exactly what's in the poison he gives Romeo, but at the time, it would probably have been a mixture of ingredients such as these:

Arsenic, a deadly mineral found in the Earth

Wolfsbane, from the roots or leaves of a well-known poisonous plant

Ground-up glass to damage the stomach and make the poison work faster

Honey to make the poison taste better

Egyptian cobra

Fun Fact!
A family of poisoners

A family named the Borgias were notorious for poisoning their way into positions of power in Italy in the 1400s, mainly using arsenic. Though it was never proved, one family member, Lucrezia Borgia, was said to have a hollow ring that she could use to secretly tip poison into her enemies' drinks.

THE LANGUAGE OF
ROMEO AND JULIET

Shakespeare's plays are mostly written in a kind of
poetry, known as blank verse. Each line of blank verse has
five stresses, or "beats", and sometimes the lines rhyme.
Shakespeare also uses poetic images to conjure up strong
feelings or a particular atmosphere, and patterns of sounds to
echo the meaning of the words. The best examples of this are
in the emotional love scenes between Romeo and Juliet.

** Simile: A simile
describes something as
being like something else.
Like Romeo if he wasn't
named Montague, a rose
without its name would be
the same thing, with the
same qualities.

Repetition: Juliet's
speech is full of
repeated words
and phrases,
emphasising
her passionate
feelings of love
and exasperation.

Metaphors: A
metaphor compares
one thing to another
by saying it *is* that
thing. Juliet says
Romeo's name is her
enemy – in fact it's
the family that has
that name.

JULIET: O Romeo, Romeo, wherefore art thou Romeo?

Deny thy father and refuse thy name.

Or if thou wilt not, be but sworn my *love

And I'll no *longer be a Capulet.

ROMEO: Shall I hear more, or shall I speak at this?

JULIET: 'Tis but thy name that is my enemy.

Thou art thyself, though not a Montague.

*Alliteration:
Pairs or groups
of words with
the same first
letter set up an
echoing pattern.

What's Montague? It is nor hand, nor foot,

Nor arm, nor face, nor any other part

Belonging to a man. O, be some other name!

What's in a name? **That which we call a rose

By any other name would *smell as *sweet.

Natural speech

Shakespeare sometimes uses more natural, everyday language too, especially for servants and informal scenes. Juliet's nurse, for example, uses blank verse when speaking to her employers. But when she's talking to Romeo in the market square, she uses more everyday language:

But first let me tell ye, if ye should lead her in a fool's paradise, as they say, it were a very gross kind of behaviour... if you should deal double with her, truly it were an ill thing

Fun Fact!
Did you know?

Many words and phrases we still use today first appeared in Shakespeare's plays, suggesting he may have invented them. In *Romeo and Juliet*, they include:

Bump   Star-crossed

Wild goose chase   Ladybird

75

WHAT *ROMEO AND JULIET* MEANS NOW

Romeo and Juliet is as popular today as it ever was. It's one of the works that people most associate with Shakespeare, and besides still being performed a lot, it has also been made into a famous ballet, an opera, songs, comic books and several films. Why do we still find something that was written more than 400 years ago so entertaining?

Young love

Romeo and Juliet are teenagers who fall hopelessly in love – and the drama and intensity of first love is something that never changes. Everyone can identify with the young lovers' passions, hopes and dreams. That's one reason why *Romeo and Juliet* is often studied in schools – it's not hard for teenagers to relate to the main characters and their feelings.

Gangs, fights and feuds

People who think gang warfare, street fights and knife crime are modern problems only have to look at *Romeo and Juliet* to see that parents and governments have been tearing their hair out over them for centuries. The Montague-Capulet battles, and Romeo's hasty revenge in which he kills Tybalt and ruins his own life, resonate with plenty of today's news stories.

Missed messages

The tragic ending of the play happens because of one disastrous detail – a message that does not get through. We all know what that's like, and feel the poor Friar's pain when he realises Romeo hasn't got his note – even if today it's more likely to be a missed text, or an email that's ended up in your spam folder, than a hand-delivered letter.

I wonder if they'll like this bit in the 21st century?

Everlasting Shakespeare

Even in Shakespeare's own time, people realised how good he was at writing about things that transcend history, and will always be important to us. After his death, another writer, Ben Jonson, praised his work, saying "He was not of an age, but for all time."

GLOSSARY

alliteration	Grouping together words with the same initial letter
apothecary	Chemist and medicine-maker
blank verse	Type of non-rhyming poetry used by Shakespeare
brawl	Rough, uncontrolled fight
dramatis personae	List of characters in a play
exile	Being thrown out of a city or country
metaphor	Describing something as another thing to compare them
playwright	Author of plays
prose	Text written in ordinary sentences, not in verse
simile	Saying something is like another thing
stage directions	Instructions for the actors in a play
supernatural	Magical or beyond the laws of nature
superstitious	Fear or belief about luck, magic or the supernatural
symbol	Something that stands for an idea or object
vault	A stone cellar for burying bodies in

GLOSSARY OF SHAKESPEARE'S LANGUAGE

art	are
baggage	immoral woman
cell	hut or small cottage
didst	did
doth	does
fie	an exclamation expressing disapproval
forfeit	penalty
forsaken	abandoned
hence	to somewhere else, over there
hie	go, travel
ill-beseeming	inappropriate
nice	polite, trivial, foolish or meaningless
thee	you
thou	you
thy	your
wherefore	why, what for
wilt	will
ye	you

ROMEO AND
JULIET QUIZ

Test yourself and your friends
on the story, characters and language
of Shakespeare's *Romeo and Juliet*.
You can find the answers at the
bottom of the page.

1) How many street fights does the Prince say have
   happened when he comes to the market square?
2) Who does Juliet dance with at the Capulet party?
3) How does Romeo get into the Capulets' orchard?
4) What time does Romeo arrange to pass on a message?
5) What does Friar Laurence grow in his garden?
6) Why does Romeo kill Tybalt?
7) What excuse does Juliet use for going to see
   the Friar again?
8) Who does Friar Laurence send to take a letter to
   Romeo?
9) What does Paris do to Juliet when he visits her
   in the vault?
10) How many people lie dead in the vault at the end?

10) *Three – Romeo, Juliet and Paris*
9) *Scatters flower petals over her*
8) *Friar John*
   to Paris
7) *To ask him to help her prepare for her wedding*
6) *Because Tybalt has killed his friend Mercutio*
5) *Herbs*
4) *Nine o'clock in the morning*
3) *He climbs over the garden wall*
2) *Count Paris*
1) *Three*

Short Sharp Shakespeare Stories

MACBETH
978 0 7502 8112 6

HAMLET
978 0 7502 8117 1

A MIDSUMMER NIGHT'S DREAM
978 0 7502 8113 3

THE TEMPEST
978 0 7502 8115 7

ROMEO AND JULIET
978 0 7502 8114 0

MUCH ADO ABOUT NOTHING
978 0 7502 8116 4